2018

The
BIG
Dessert Book
for Children

By Chef Carl Thomas

AuthorHouse™
1663 Liberty Drive
Bloomington, IN 47403
www.authorhouse.com
Phone: 1 (800) 839-8640

Published by AuthorHouse 10/17/2018

ISBN: 978-1-5462-6384-5(sc)
ISBN: 978-1-5462-6385-2 (e)

Library of Congress Control Number: 2018912306

Print information available on the last page.

authorHOUSE®

About the Author

My name is Pastry chef Carl Thomas, and I taught myself how to bake. I was born and raised in Buffalo, New York. I am the fourth child out of five children. I chose to write a cook book just for children of any age to teach a person how to bake. I took classes at Michael's craft store. The first course I took was the discover cake decorating. Also, the second class I took classes was the Wilton Method of Cake Decorating Flowers and Borders. The third course I took was Fondant and Tiered Cakes. The fourth class I took was the Fondant and Gum Paste. It took me four months to complete the courses. When a child is baking, make sure the parents are around to help and assist

About the Book

This book is about children baking desserts at any age. Make sure everyone follows directions while baking these recipes. Make sure that there is always a parent supervising while baking in a cooking area.

Chef Carl Thomas
Caramel cake/ Cupcake

Ingredients

2/3 Cup. Land O lake butter softened
1 1/3 Cup. Domino sugar
3 eggs. Egg-land
2 ¼ Cup. Silk cake flour
½ tsp. Clabber Girl baking powder
2/3 Cup. Upstate Farm whole milk
1 tsp. McCormick vanilla extract

In a large bowl put butter, pure sugar cane, vanilla extract put mixer on medium speed. In another bowl add flour, baking powder whisk dry ingredients together put dry ingredients with the wet ingredients use the milk also. Spray each baking pans Wilton baking spray if not just put some vegetable oil in the cake pan. Bake cake at 350 degrees in the oven for 25 to 30 minutes insert a wooded toothpick in the center if it comes out clean then the cake is done take out and let it cool on a wire rack for 15 minutes.

Caramel frosting

1 Cup. Domino sugar about
¼ Cup. Water

4 egg white's eggs-land
1 Cup. Domino confectioner's sugar
1 Cup (2 sticks) Land O lake butter, softened
1 teaspoon McCormick vanilla extract

Combine the sugar in a saucepan with enough water to make "wet sand." Cook on medium high heat, not stirring, until the sugar is a deep golden color. Remove from the heat and allow to cool for 2 to 3 minutes.

While the sugar is cooking, whip the eggs whites, adding confectioners' sugar in Stage 3 after the eggs being to form, to soft peak. With the mixer running, slowly pour in the sugar. Whip until the mixture is cooled. Cut the butter into small pieces and add them, a few at a time, with the mixer running. Add the vanilla.

You also can use this frosting for cupcakes.

Caramel Vanilla Chai Tea Velvet Cake/ Cupcakes also

2 ½ Cup Silk cake flour
1 ½ cup Domino sugar
1 ½ Cup Crisco oil
1 Cup Butter milk
2 eggs
1 tsp McCormick pure vanilla extract
2 tsp Caramel Vanilla Chai Tea mix
1 tsp salt
1 tsp baking soda
1 tsp white vinegar

Combine all dry ingredients in one bowl cake flour, Chai tea, baking soda, salt. Combine all wet ingredients in another bowl Domino sugar, McCormick pure vanilla extract, vinegar, eggs, Crisco oil. Pour batter into, 2 9-inch spray cake pan with Wilton baking spray put oven on 350 degrees bake the cakes for 30-35 minutes inserted a wooden toothpick in the center comes out clean take the cakes out and let cool for about 15 minutes on a wire rack.

Cream cheese frosting

1 Box (16oz) Domino confectioner's sugar (sifted)
1 stick Land o lake butter

18oz package of cream cheese
1 tsp McCormick pure vanilla extract
1 cup of mixed nuts (Optional)

Combine first 5 ingredients. Add remaining ingredients until icing forms peaks. Fold in the nuts and spread over the cake.

Lemon Curd Bars

Crust

1.5 cups all purposes flour
¼ cup D0mino powder sugar
12 tbsp. (1.5 sticks of butter) cut into small pieces
Filling
6 eggs
3 cups of Domino sugar
Grated zest of 1 lemon
1 cup plus 2 tablespoons lemon juice
½ cup all purposes flour

Preheat oven to 325 degrees. Have rack in the middle of oven. Have ready a 13x9 baking pan. Stir together 1.5 cups of flour and powdered sugar in a large bowl. Sprinkle butter over the top. Using a pastry blender or your fingertips cut in the mixture until the mixture is the size of small peas. Using your fingers press the mixture into the bottom of the pan and ¾ of the way up the sides. Bake until golden brown, 20~30 minutes. Set aside to cool slightly. Reduce oven temperature to 300 degrees. Whisk together until well combined the eggs and sugar. Stir in zest and lemon juice. Sift over the top and stir until well blended the ½ cup of flour. Pour the batter over the baked crust. Bake until set (about 35 minutes) Remove from oven and let cool completely before cutting into squares.

Makes 18 3x2″ Bars.

Carl C's Pies

Ingredients

1 Cup. Land O Lake butter softened
2 Cups Domino sugar
2 eggs
2 tsp. McCormick vanilla extract
4 Cups. Pillsbury flour
1 Cup. Hershey's cocoa
3 tsp. soda
1 tsp. Clabber Girl baking powder
1 tsp. salt
2 Cups. Any type of milk

Cream the butter, sugar, eggs and vanilla. In a separate bowl, mix the dry ingredients. Add milk to the creamed mixture and well. Add the blended dry ingredients mix well again. Drop by teaspoonfuls on ungreased cookie sheet and bake at 350 degrees for 7 to 8 minutes. Cool, then fill.

Whoopie Pie Filling:

1 Cup. Crisco shortening
1 ½ tsp McCormick vanilla extract

Sm. Amount of milk
1 sm. Jar Marshmallow crème
1 (lb.) Box of Domino confectioner's sugar

Cream the shortening, sugar, vanilla. Add the marshmallow crème and cream again, adding milk as necessary. This makes enough

Filling to generously fill approximately 50 whoopie pies (3-inch size).

Carl Famous Fudge

Ingredients

5 Cup. Domino sugar
1 can Carnation evaporated milk (12 oz.) you only need (10 oz.)
12 oz. Semi-sweet chocolate chips
2 tsp. McCormick vanilla extract
4 Tbsp. Land O lake butter
2 Cups. Chopped walnuts (opt.)

Combine: together sugar and evaporated milk in a non-stick pot. Mixture will be very thick. Cook on low heat and watch closely until its beings to boil. Let come to full rolling boil. Then boil exactly for 6 minutes. Remove from heat. Then add chocolate chips, bearing until melted and smooth. Mix in butter and vanilla by hand. Last mix in chopped nuts (opt). Pour into buttered firm rapidly. 4 pounds.

Carl Thomas Pie Crust

Ingredients:

3 Sticks Land O lake butter use cold butter cut into pieces
3 Cups. Pillsbury flour
1 Tsp. Salt
1 Tbsp. Domino sugar
Ice cold water

Combine: flour, salt, sugar in a medium bowl whisk together. Put mixture in the food processor turn machine on throw. Cut pieces of butter into the machine. Add cold water not a lot just enough to form a ball. Take out the dough an put it in plastic wrap put in the refrigerator for 30 minutes then take dough out. Put flour on the board and roll the pie crust out.

Carl's famous three flavor cake

Ingredients

2 cups. Domino pure cane sugar
1 tsp. McCormick Coconut extract, butter extract, vanilla extract
3 ½ Cups. Silk cake flour
3 egg-land eggs
3 tsp. Clabber Girl baking powder
1 ¼ Upstate Farm whole milk
3 (sticks) of Land O lake butter
Preheat oven to 350 degrees

To grease cake pans, use Wilton baking spray it is a very great product to use. In a large bowl use an electric mixer on medium speed. Cream butter, sugar, eggs one at a time wet ingredient. In a medium bowl combine flour, baking powder dry ingredients. Add milk in between mixing, pour cake batter into the greased baking pans.

Bake at 350 degrees for 30 to 35 minutes. Insert a wooden toothpick in the center if toothpick come out clean take the cakes out and let cool on a wire rack for 10 to 15 minutes,

Glaze icing for Pound Cake also for a 2-layer cake.

1 Cup. Domino confectioners' sugar
½ Cup. Upstate Farm whole milk
1 tsp. McCormick lemon extract, butter extract, vanilla extract.

Mix in a large bowl confectioners' sugar, milk, lemon extract, butter extract, vanilla extract with a whisk until smooth than spread glaze on one than spread glaze on the second layer and make sure you are icing the sides.

It can serve about 8 to 10 people

Cheese Cake

Crust:

1 Cup. Vanilla Wafers
3 Tsp. Domino sugar
3 Tsp. Land O lake butter
Use springform pan for the crust.

Filling:

4 pack of Philadelphia cream cheese, Mascarpone cream cheese
1 Cup. Domino sugar
3 Tbsp. Pillsbury flour
1 Tbsp. McCormick lemon extract
1 Cup. Daily sour cheese
4 egg-land eggs

Ingredients:

Combine cream cheese, sugar, flour, lemon extract, sour cream, eggs use a large bowl an electric mixer on medium speed. Put oven on 325 degrees for 65 to 70 minutes insert a wooden toothpick in the center if it comes out clean it is done put on wire rack and let cool. Get a nice cake plate after cool unlatch the springform pan.

Chef Carl Thomas
Crème Brulee

Ingredients

3 slightly beaten eggs
2 Cups. Upstate Farm light cream
¼ Cup. Domino sugar
¼ tsp. salt
½ tsp. McCormick vanilla extract
½ Cup. Domino packed brown sugar

In a heavy 2-quart saucepan combine the first 4 ingredients. Cook and stir over medium heat, about 15 minutes or until it coats a back of wooden spoon. Remove from heat.

Pour into 1-quart baking dish and place in a pan of ice water for 2 ½ hours. Press brown sugar through a sieve over the custard. Set baking dish in pan of ice cubes and cold water. Place under broiler 4-5 inches from heat. Broil 1 to 2 minutes or until the brown sugar turns golden brown and a bubby crust form. Serve either warm or chilled.

Makes 6 servings.

Oatmeal Raisin Cookies

Ingredients

1 cup (2 sticks) Land o Lake butter, softened
1 cup Domino sugar
2/3 cup Domino firmly packed light brown sugar
2 tsp McCormick vanilla extract
2 large eggs
1 ½ Pillsbury all- purpose flour
1 tsp baking soda
½ tsp salt
3 cups oatmeal
¾ cup raisin

Preheat oven to 350 degrees. Line baking sheets with parchment paper/ silicone mat.

Mix butter, sugar, light brown sugar, vanilla, eggs in a large bowl. Beat with an electric mixer on high speed until fluffy. Combine Pillsbury flour, baking soda and salt in a medium bowl, beat into butter mixture on low speed. Stir in rolled oats and raisin until well blended. Drop dough by heaping tablespoonful about 3 inches apart on prepared parchment paper. Bake until golden, 10-15 minutes. Transfer cookies to wire rack to cool.

Makes 3 dozen cookies

From Generation to Generation handed down Great Egg Pie

Ingredients

½ Cup. Domino sugar
2 eggs. Use great value eggs
1 tsp. Pillsbury all-purpose flour
2 Blocks. of Land O Lake butter or margarine
1 tsp. McCormick Lemon extract
1 can of Carnation evaporation milk
Pinch of salt
1 Deep dish pie crust already rolled Tops brand

Combine sugar, eggs, flour, extract, butter, milk in a large bowl mix with a whisk. Roll crust output in pie pan.

Bake pie for 1 hour on 350 degrees then for the last 15 minutes turn it down to 300 degrees for the remaining time.

When the middle is firm and golden brown that mean it is time to take it out set it on a wire rack to cool.

Make sure your parents are showing you make a very special pie.

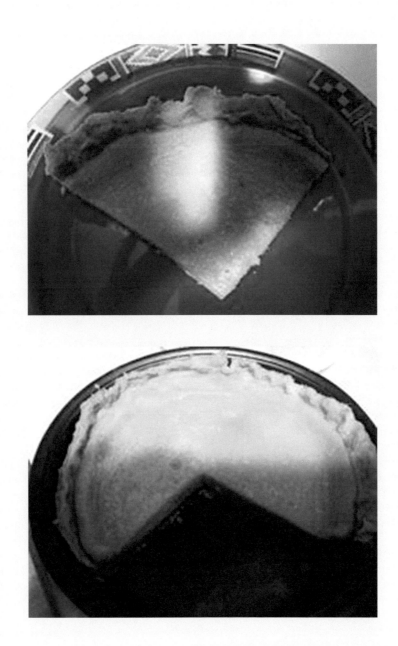

Chef Thomas Moose Balls

Ingredients

18-ounce regular Oreo cookies (not double filled)
8 ounces cream cheese
12 ounces Toll house chocolate chips

Preparation method

Use a food processor to mix ingredients, leave cream cheese out on the counter overnight it will be soft about time you get ready to use it. Melted chocolate chips in a double boiler or microwave oven.

Combine: Cream cheese, Oreo cookies break Oreo cookies in small pieces or large chunks depending on how you like your balls. Mix Oreo cookies, cream cheese it should be the sizes of a toonie and place in the refrigerator for about 1 hour to firm up. Melted chocolate in a double boiler on stove top or use a microwave. Remove balls from the refrigerator and quickly roll the prepared balls in the melted chocolate. You must do this step quickly as chocolate will being to stiffer because of the chilled balls. Place balls on a baking sheet pan covered in parchment paper and return to the refrigerator or freezer to firm up chocolate.

Makes 20 to 25 balls

Chewy Chocolate Cookies

4 egg-land egg whites
2 ½ Cups. Domino confectioners' sugar
1 Cup. Hersey unsweetened cocoa powder
2 Tbsp. Pillsbury flour/ Pastry flour
1 Tsp. instant coffee/ espresso coffee powder
1 Tbsp. water
1 Cup. Walnuts finely chopped (0pt)

1. Preheat the oven to 350 degrees, line 2 cookie sheets with wax paper and use Wilton baking spray on the paper.
2. With an electric mixer, beat the egg whites until frothy.
3. Sift the sugar, cocoa, flour, and coffee espresso into the whites. Add the water and continue beating on low speed to blend then on high for a few minutes until mixture thickens. With a rubbers spatula fold in the Walnuts (opt).
4. Place generous spoonsful of the mixture 1 inches apart on the prepared sheets.
5. Bake until firm and cracked on top but soft on the inside, 12-15 minutes. With a metal spatula, transfer to a wire rack to cool.

-Variation-

If wished, Add ½ Cup. chocolate chips to the dough with nuts.

Christmas Cookies

Ingredients

½ Cup. Land O Lake butter (1 stick) unsalted
1 ½ Cup. Firmly packed light brown sugar
2 eggs
1 Cup. dairy sour cream
1 tsp. McCormick vanilla extract
2 ¼ Cup. All-purpose flour (1/2 Cup. Extra)
1 tsp baking soda
1 tsp Clabber Girl baking powder
½ tsp salt

Preparation

In bowl cream butter gradually. Add sugar, beat until fluffy and light. Blend in sour cream and vanilla. Sift together dry ingredients. Gradually add all together. Bake at 350 degrees for 8 to 10 minutes.

Icing

½ Cup. Butter
3 ½ Cup. Powder sugar
1 tsp. vanilla extract
¼ tsp. salt

Cream Cheese Spirals

Crust

1 Cup. (2 sticks) Land O lakes butter at room temperature
8 oz cream cheese
2 Tsp. Domino pure cane sugar
2 Cups. Pillsbury flour
1 egg-land egg white beaten with 1 tbsp water for glazing
Domino sugar is for sprinkling on the dough

For the filling

1 Cup. walnuts, pecans finely chopped
½ Cup. Domino light brown sugar finely packed
1 Tsp. McCormick ground cinnamon

1. Preheat the oven at 375 degrees. Use 2 pieces of parchments paper on cookie sheets
2. With an electric mixer, in a large bowl cream butter and cream cheese and sugar until soft. Sift over the flour and mix to form a dough. Gather into a ball and divide in half. Flatten each half, wrap it in wax paper and refrigerate for at least 30 minutes.
3. Meanwhile make the filling. Mix together the chopped walnuts, pecans in the light brown sugar and the cinnamon set a side.

4. Working with one half of the dough at a time, roll out thinly into a circle about 11 inches in diameter. Trim the edges with a knife, using a dinner plate as a guide.
5. Brush the surface with the egg white glaze and sprinkle the dough evenly with half the filling.
6. Cut the dough into quarters into 4 sections, to form 16 triangles.
7. Starting from the base of the triangles, roll up to form spirals.
8. Place on the sheet pan and brush with the remaining glaze. Sprinkle with Domino sugar bake until golden brown for 15-20 minutes. Cool on wire rack
9. Make sure you make this with your family on any giving morning, afternoon, and evening and snack.

Cream- Filled Strawberries

Ingredients

18 Jumbo Strawberries

1 Cup. Heavy cream

1 package vanilla flavoring instant pudding and pie filling for 4 serving

1 Cup Upstate Farm milk

1 teaspoon McCormick vanilla extract

Preparation method

In an electric mixer beat 1 Cup of cream over high speed until stiff peaks form. In a large bowl with wire whisk, prepare instant pudding as per label directions but use only 1 Cup of milk. With a rubber spatula, gently fold whipped cream and vanilla extract into prepared instant pudding mix. new spoon formed vanilla cream mixture into a decorative pipping bag with large star tip. Next, cut stems off strawberries and save for plate garnish if desired. With a sharp paring knife cut an "X" in the top of each strawberry about two – thirds of the way down. With fingertip's gently spread each strawberry apart to make "petals." Pipe cream mixture in center of strawberries. Cover and refrigerate or use immediately. Serving 3 strawberries as a dessert serving.

Makes 6 servings.

Death by Chocolate Cake

Ingredients

3 ½ Cup. Silk cake flour

2 Cup. Domino sugar

3 (Stick of butter) Land O lakes butter

3 egg-land eggs

2 Tsp. McCormick lemon extract

2 Tsp. Hershey's cocoa

3 Tsp. Clabber Girl baking powder

1 Tsp. salt

1 ¼ Cup. Upstate Farm butter milk

Combine: wet ingredients in a large bowl cream butter, sugar, eggs, lemon extract. Put the eggs in one at time. Use an electric mixer on medium speed then another bowl combines dry ingredients flour, salt, baking powder, cocoa and use a whisk together than put dry ingredients with wet ingredients make sure you put the milk in also then mix all the ingredients. Take two cake pans you can use Pam baking spray or Wilton baking spray that is very good for baking. Put the oven on 350 degrees and bake the cakes for about 30 to 35 minutes until done. Make sure you use a wooden toothpick to insert in the center if the toothpick come out clean take the cake pans out and let cool on a wire rack 10 minutes. While cakes are cooling make the chocolate frosting.

Death by Chocolate Cake Frosting

Ingredients:

1 Stick (½) Land O lakes butter
2/3 Cup. Hersey's cocoa powder
3 Cup. Domino confectioners' sugar
1/3 Cup. Upstate Farm milk
1 Tsp. McCormick lemon extract

In a large bowl mix together butter, cocoa powder, powder sugar, lemon extract, and milk. Use an electric mixer on low speed put 1 cup at a time with the powder sugar also use the milk. Keep mixer on low speed until frosting is fluffy and smooth after the cake cool spread frosting on 1 layer put other layer on and spread frosting on top layer then do the sides cut and serve. Enjoy what you bake, practice this cake and you will get better each time you use this recipe, make sure your grandparents, and parents make the cake with you.

Flan (Mexican Custard)

Ingredients

1 can Carnation evaporated milk
1 can Carnation condensed milk
1 tbsp McCormick vanilla extract
4 eggs
¼ Cup. Domino sugar

Melt sugar in a skillet until light brown, pour in a pie pan (glass). Blend milk, eggs and vanilla (don't over blend), pour into pie pan. Put glass pie dish into a large baking pan. Pour water in baking pan so the dish can set in the water while cooking. Spray pan with Wilton baking spray.

Bake at 325 degrees for one hour, let cool and refrigerate. Caramel on the bottom will running.

Fresh Blueberry Muffin

Ingredients

1 ½ Cups. fresh blueberry or frozen blueberry
2 Cups. Pillsbury all-purpose flour divided
½ Cup. Domino sugar
1 tbsp. Clabber Girl baking powder
½. Salt
1 Large egg-land egg
1 Cup. upstate milk
¼ Cup. (1/2 stick) Land O lake butter melted

Prepare

- Preheat oven 400 degrees. Don't forget to grease the muffin pan or just use cupcake tins or use Wilton baking spray.
- Mix blueberries with 1 tablespoon flour, set aside.
- Combine remaining flour, sugar, baking powder and salt in a large mixing bowl.
- Mix egg, milk and melted butter in another bowl. Stir egg mixture into dry ingredients until just combined. Gently stir in blueberries.
- Scoop batter into prepared muffin cups.

  Makes 1 dozen of muffin

Lemon Pound Cake

Ingredients

    3 stick land o lake butter
    3 eggs
    3 ½ silk cake flour
    2 tsp. McCormick vanilla extract
    3 tsp. Baking powder
    2 Cups. Domino sugar
    1 ¼ Cup. Milk

Combine butter, eggs, sugar, vanilla extract, in a lager bowl using an electric mixer medium speed in another bowl combine cake flour, baking powder whisk together dry ingredients, put dry ingredients with the wet ingredients mix together on low speed use the milk also. Put oven on 350 degrees and bake for 1 hour or insert a toothpick in the center of the cake place it on wire rack to cool for 10 minutes then spread the icing on the top of the cake.

Lemon icing

    1 Cup. Domino confectioner's sugar
    1 tsp. McCormick lemon extract
    2 tablespoon Land O Lake butter
    ½ Milk
    1 tsp. Lemon juice

Combine butter, confectioner's sugar, lemon extract, milk, lemon juice uses electric mixer until creamy.

Carl's Brownies

Ingredients

4 Tbsp. Land O lake butter at room temperature
6 oz. Philadelphia cream cheese
½ Cup. Domino sugar
2 egg-land eggs
2 Tbsp. Pillsbury flour
1 Tsp. McCormick pure vanilla extract

Combine: wet ingredients butter, cream cheese, sugar, eggs, vanilla extract. Mix with electric mixer. Add flour mix until fluffy. Spray a 9x9 – inch square baking pan with Wilton baking spray pour batter into the pan and put the oven on 350 degrees bake for 35-40 minutes inserted a toothpick in the center if it comes out clean it is done. Let it cool for 20 minutes than cut into square. You can double the recipes, make sure you do this recipe with your parents, grandparents, uncle, aunt.

Makes 24

Orange Doughnuts

Ingredients

2 tbsp. Land O lake butter
1 Cup. Domino sugar
2 large egg-land eggs
1 tbsp. grated orange rind
4 Cups. Pastry flour
½ tsp. salt
2 tsp. Clabber Girl baking powder
¾ tsp. baking soda
¾ Cup. Orange juice
1 Cup. Domino Confectioner's sugar

Preparation method

In a large bowl cream butter, sugar, eggs, and wet ingredients. In another bowl is dry ingredients flour, baking soda, salt, baking powder, combine with orange juices use an electric mixer on high speed with dough hooks. Chill dough in refrigerator for about 3 hours or enough to roll dough out. Roll dough ½ to ¾ inch thick and cut with a floured doughnut cutter. Let the doughnuts stand while the fat heats. Fry at 375 degrees turn once. Shake it in a bag with I Cup. Domino confectioner's sugar and 1 tbsp grated rind.

Peanut Butter Cake

Ingredients:

1 box yellow Pillsbury cake mix, follow directions on the box
¾ Cup. Peter pan peanut butter
2 Tbsp. Domino confectioners' sugar

Mix cake according to directions on box and add peanut butter, confectioners' sugar. Mix well make sure you used Wilton baking spray. Bake put oven on 350 degrees until done inserted wooden toothpick come out clean cake is done. Let cake cool on a wire rack for 15 minutes.

Peanut butter frosting

Ingredients:

1/3 Cup. Pillsbury all-purpose flour plus 2 Tbsp flour
Dash of salt
1 Cup. milk
½ Cup. Crisco sold stick
½ Cup. Land O lake butter (1 stick) softened
1 ¼ Cup. Domino sugar
1 Tsp. McCormick vanilla extract

½ Cup. Peter pan peanut butter
2/3 Tbsp. Domino confectioners' powder sugar} add this last

1. Combine: flour, salt in 2-quart saucepan. Gradually stir in milk until well blended. Cook over medium heat until thickened, stirring constantly. Cool.
2. Beat together Crisco shorting mix in a large bowl with electric mixer at medium speed until creamy. Add sugar, beat until light and fluffy.
3. Blend in vanilla. Add cooled flour mixture, beat until smooth.

Peanut Butter Pie

Ingredients

1 (8oz.) pkg. Philadelphia cream cheese
1 Cup. Domino powder sugar
½ Creamy Peter Pan peanut butter
6 (40z) Graham cracker crust
1 (80z) containers cool whip

Preparation

Mix cream cheese, peanut butter with spoon or spatula. Add sugar and mix. Add 1 topping and whip until fluffy with mixer. Put into pie shell and cover with rest of topping. Chill in refrigerator until ready to serve.

Make this recipe with your parents and grandparents.

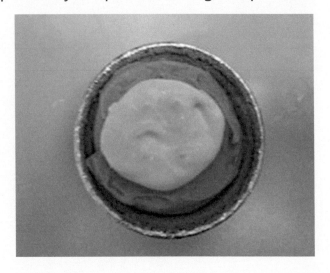

Pecan and Walnuts Pie

Ingredients:

1 (9inch) pie crust
3 Egg-land eggs lightly beaten
1 Cup. Domino sugar
1 Cup. Karo light corn syrup
3 Tbsp. Land O lake butter
1 Tsp. McCormick vanilla extract
1 Cup. broken pecans
1 unbaked 9-inch pie crust
10-12 pecan halves

Combine: eggs, sugar, corn syrup, butter, vanilla extract, and pecan pieces. Pour filling into prepared pie crust. Arrange pecan halves around the inside edge. Bake at 400 degrees for 10 minutes. Reduce heat to 350 degrees. Bake 40 minutes longer or until the center is firm. Cool before serving.

Pecan Tessie's

Dough

    4oz. Philadelphia cream cheese
    ½ Cup. (1stick) Land O Lake butter
    1 Cup. Pastry flour

For the dough use a food processor on low speed combine cream cheese, butter, flour. Cut the cream cheese and butter in pieces, put in the food processor on low speed after the butter than put the pastry flour. Roll the dough out on flour counter thinly with a flited pastry cutter, stamps out 24 2 ½-inch rounds. Use Wilton baking spray for the muffin tin pan than line the muffin cups with the round cut outs than refrigerate while making the filling.

Put oven on 350 degrees, Use Wilton baking spray for muffin tins.

For the filling

Ingredients:

    2 egg-land eggs
    ¾ Cup. Domino dark brown sugar, firmly packed
    1 Tsp. McCormick vanilla extract
    1/8 Tsp. salt
    2 Tbsp. Land O Lake butter melted
    1 Cup. pecans (opt)

For the filling. In a medium bowl whisk together eggs, brown sugar, butter, salt, vanilla extract and set aside.

Reserve 24 undamaged pecan halves and chop the rest coarsely with a sharp chef knife make sure your parents are in the kitchen when you chop the nuts.

Add chop pecans to the filling and take a spoonful of the mixture in muffin cups bake for 15 to 20 minutes insert wooden toothpick in the center if it comes out clean it would be done take out the oven and transfer to a wire rack to cool for 10 minutes.

-Variation-

To make jam Tessie's, fill the cream cheese pastry shells with raspberry or blackberry jam or other fruit jam. Bake as described.

Real Lemon and Blueberries Tea Muffins

Ingredients

1 Pint Blueberries
3 Cup. Pillsbury flour
2 Tsp. Clabber Girl baking powder
1 Cup. Land O lake butter
1 Lemon, grated (rind)
4 Land O lake eggs beaten
1 Cup. Upstate Farm milk
1 Cup. chopped walnuts (opt) or 1 cup. chopped pecans (opt)
1 Tsp. salt
1 Lemon, grated (rind)
1 Cup. Domino sugar

In a medium bowl add flour, baking powder, and salt whisk together. Cream butter and sugar and add 1 lemon rind. Cream until light and fluffy. Beat in eggs. Add dry ingredients alternately with milk. Stir in nuts (opt).

Mix together 1 lemon rind and 1 Cup sugar and sprinkle on top. Bake at 375 degrees for 20-25 minutes.

Makes 20.

Red Velvet Brownies

Ingredients

1 stick Land O lake butter
1 Cup. Domino pure cane sugar
1 tsp. McCormick vanilla extract
¼ Cup. Hersey cocoa powder
Pinch of salt
1 tsp. Red Food Coloring
1 tsp. White vinegar
2 egg-land eggs
¾ Cup. Pillsbury all-purpose flour
¼ Cup. Chopped toasted walnuts (optional)

In a large bowl cream butter and sugar with an electric mixer on high speed. Add eggs one at a time add vanilla, vinegar. In another bowl add flour, salt, cocoa. Toasted nuts (optional). Put oven on 350 degrees bake for 30 minutes. Let cool on a wire rack for 10 to 15 minutes then cut the brownies into squares.

Cream Cheese Icing

Ingredients

8 oz Philadelphia cream cheese
¼ Cup. Domino sugar
1 egg-land egg
1/8 tsp. McCormick vanilla extract

In a large bowl mix cream cheese and sugar, egg, vanilla extract mix with an electric mixer medium speed until well mix. PUT cream cheese icing on the top of the brownie.

Orange Velvet Cake/ Red Velvet Cake also

Ingredients

3 ½ Cup Silk cake flour
2 Cup Domino sugar
3 stick Land o lake butter
1 1/4 Cup Upstate Farm butter milk
3 eggs
2 tsp McCormick vanilla extract
2 tsp Hershey's cocoa
1 tsp salt
3 tsp baking soda
1 tsp vinegar
2 drops of Ameri Color, Soft Gel Paste Food Color Orange or 2 drops of
Red food coloring.

Combine wet ingredients in a large bowl sugar, eggs, butter, vinegar mix
with electric mixer then in another bowl mix dry ingredients combine flour,
baking soda, cocoa powder, salt whist together and pour butter milk and
put mixer on low do not over beat it. Spray baking pans with Wilton baking
spray. Put the oven on 350 degrees for 30 to 35 minutes.

Icing:

2 drops orange food coloring
2 Cups Domino powder sugar
1 stick Land o lake butter softened
1 8-ounce Philadelphia cream cheese
1 tsp McCormick vanilla extract
1 Cup Walnuts, Pecans (opt)
Combine powder sugar, butter, cream cheese, vanilla extract. F

Red Velvet cookies

Ingredients:

1 1/3 Cup. Pillsbury all-purpose flour
2 Tsp. Hersey cocoa powder
1 Tsp. Clabber Girl baking powder
¼ Cup. baking soda
¼ Cup. Land O lake butter at room temperature
1 Cup. Domino pure cane sugar
2 egg-land eggs
2 Tsp. Upstate Farm buttermilk
2 Tsp. Apple cider vinegar
1 Tsp. McCormick vanilla extract
1 Tsp. red food coloring

In a large bowl put wet ingredients cream butter, sugar eggs, lemon extract leave red food coloring for last. Use an electric mixer on medium speed. Put dry ingredients together flour, cocoa powder, baking powder, baking soda, salt put all ingredients in the same bowl mix together pour buttermilk and food coloring in the batter until buttermilk is all in the batter. Preheat oven on 350 degrees bake for 15 minutes until bake through. Let cool on a wire rack for 10 minutes.

Cream cheese frosting

1 8oz pack Philadelphia cream cheese
1 stick Land O lake butter
1 Tsp. McCormick vanilla extract
1 box Domino confectioners' powder sugar
¾ Cup. finely chopped nuts walnuts, pecans (opt.)

Use electric mixer, in a large bowl add cream cheese, butter, powder sugar, vanilla extract, nuts.

Sesame Cookies

Ingredients

1 Cups. Of Pillsbury flour another 1 Cup Pastry flour 2 cup of flour
1½ Tsp. Clabber Girl baking powder
½ Tsp. Salt
2/3 Cup. Domino sugar
2/3 Cup. Land O lake butter
2 egg substitutes, lightly beaten
1 Tbsp. Upstate Farm low-fat milk
1 Tsp. McCormick vanilla extract
2 ½ Tbsp. sesame seeds

In a medium bowl combine flour, baking powder, and salt whisk dry ingredients together. In another bowl cream butter, sugar wet ingredients. While mixing, add beaten egg substitutes, milk and vanilla to sugar-butter mixture. Gradually stir in dry ingredients.

Preheat oven to 350 degrees. Bake for 10-15 minutes if not done put back in the oven for 5 more minutes. Let cool in pan on a wire rack.

Sugar Cookies (Cutouts)

Ingredients

1 Cup. Land o lake butter
1 ½ Cup. Domino sugar
3 egg. Land eggs beaten well
1 tsp. McCormick vanilla extract
3 ½ Cup. all-purpose flour/ Pastry flour
2 tsp. McCormick cream of tartar
1 tsp. Baking soda
½ tsp. salt

Combine wet ingredients sugar, butter, vanilla, eggs in a large bowl mix with electric mixer. Combine dry ingredients in another bowl whist flour, cream tartar, baking soda, salt blend together well. Add dry ingredients to wet ingredients mix and chill. Put oven on 350 degrees for 10 minutes.

Butter cream icing

Please pay close attention to the recipe on how to make butter cream icing.
1 Cup. Solid Crisco shortening
1 tsp. McCormick vanilla, lemon extract

2 tablespoons. Milk, water
2 Cups. Domino confectioner's sugar
1 Tablespoon Wilton Meringue powder
A pinch of salt (optional)

McCormick flavors may give you a better taste than any other flavors to suit your taste.

Cream shortening, flavoring and milk. Add dry ingredients and mix on medium speed until all ingredients have been thoroughly mixed together. Blend an additional minute or until creamy.

Stiff consistency is used for decorations such as flowers with upright petals like roses and sweet peas.

Medium consistency creates stems, figure piping, borders and flowers with petals that lie flat. Add 1 tsp water milk to each cup of stiff consistency icing (1 additional tablespoon of milk or water when using the full recipe). Mix until well blend.

Sweet Potatoes Pie

Ingredients

2 Cup. Domino sugar
4 egg-land eggs
1 stick Land o lake butter
2 Tsp. McCormick lemon extract
1 Tsp. cinnamon
1 Tsp. nutmeg
4 Tbsp. milk
3 big Sweet Potatoes

I need 1 large pot, make sure you peel the potatoes before you put them in the pot. Let the potatoes cook until fork tender drains the water after they are done, leave the potatoes in the pot use an electric to take the string out the Potatoes so it looks smooth. Put the oven at 350 degrees for 10 minutes reduce to 325 degrees for the remaining 45 minutes back to the ingredients add sugar, eggs, butter, lemon extract, cinnamon, nutmeg, milk use an electric mixer to mix all the ingredients.

You also can purchase deep dish pie crust or make yours from scratch in a food processor. I have a tart shell recipe in this book will make this Sweet Potatoes pie taste great.

Tart Shells Also can use this Tart shell with Lemon square filling
Is
Filled with sauté Onions, Garlic, Spinach and Coble Jack
cheese with ground chicken and ground turkey.

Ingredients

2 Cup. Pillsbury flour
½ tsp. salt
2/3 Cup. Crisco shortening
¼ Cup. plus 2 tbsp. water

Combine flour and salt in a mixing bowl; cut in shortening with a pastry blender until mixture resembles coarse meal. Sprinkle water evenly over surface. Stir with a fork until dry and ingredients are moistened. Shape dough into a ball. Chill as directed in desired recipe. Roll dough out use a round cookie cutter then put in a tin baking pan. Put oven on 325 degrees for about 10-15 minutes until golden brown let them cool on a wire rack, fill them with the filling you made earlier.

Ingredients

2 Large onions
½ bag of spinach
1 tbsp of garlic
1 Cup of cheese
3 pinches of kosher salt

3 pinches of black pepper
¼ Cup of Extra Virgin Olive oil

Heat a large sauté pan on medium heat. Pour olive oil in pan, sauté onions, garlic, spinach, salt, black pepper put cheese in last set it aside.

Heat a large sauté pan on medium heat. Combine ground chicken and ground turkey also season it with black pepper and salt garlic powder, onion powder for taste.

Vanilla Wafers recipe

Ingredients

½ Cup. Land O Lake butter softened
1 Cup. Domino sugar
1 egg
1 tablespoon McCormick vanilla extract
1 1/3 Cup. All-purpose flour/ Pastry flour
¾ teaspoon baking powder
¼ teaspoon salt

Preheat oven to 350 degrees F (175 degrees C). Beat butter, sugar, egg, vanilla extract, in a lager bowl use electric mixer on high speed until light and fluffy. Combine flour, baking powder, salt whist together in another bowl put dry ingredients with wet ingredients use electric mixer on low speed. Use parchment paper or silicone for cookie sheet pan. Drop Cookies about 2 inches apart 1 tsp at a time, onto ungreased baking sheet. Bake in preheat oven until edges of cookies are golden brown for about 12 to 15 minutes take out and let cool on a wire rack.

Zucchini Bread

Ingredients

3.25 Cups. All-purpose flour/ Pastry flour
1.5 tsp. Salt
1 tsp. McCormick nutmeg
2 tsp. Baking soda
3 Cups. Domino sugar
1 Cup. Crisco oil
4 eggs beaten
1/3 Cup. Zucchini juice
2 Cups. Shredded zucchini
1 tsp. lemon juice
1 Cup. Chopped Walnuts/ Pecans (opt)

Preparation Method

Preheat oven to 350 degrees. In a large bowl combine flour, salt, nutmeg, baking soda, cinnamon, and sugar. In a separate bowl combine oil, eggs, zucchini juice, shredded zucchini, and lemon juice. Mix wet ingredients into dry. Add nuts and fold in. Bake in 2 standard loaf pans spray with Wilton nonstick baking spray. For 1 hour until you insert a toothpick in the center comes out clean. Alternately, bake in 2 loaf pans for about 45 minutes. Make 2 9x5 loaves

Zucchini Cookies

Ingredients:

1 cup. Domino sugar
½ Cup. (low fat) butter
¼ Cup. egg-land egg substitutes
1 Tsp. McCormick vanilla extract
1 ½ Cup. Pillsbury flour
½ Tsp. salt
½ Tsp. clabber girl baking powder
½ Tsp. Arm & baking soda
½ Tsp. McCormick cinnamon
¼ Tsp. McCormick cloves
¼ Tsp. McCormick nutmeg

Use an electric mixer put it on medium speed with dough hooks.

Wet ingredients combine sugar, eggs, vanilla extract in a large bowl in another bowl combine dry ingredients flour, salt, baking powder, baking soda, cinnamon, cloves, nutmeg.

Add:

1 ½ Cup. Oatmeal
1 Cup. Grated, drained zucchini
½ Cup. Chopped nuts (optional)
½ Cup. Raisins (optional)

Drop by tablespoons on Wilton baking sprayed greased cookies sheet. Bake at 350 degrees for 10-12 minutes or until lightly browned.

Make these cookies for anyone that wants to eat health. Bake some homemade zucchini cookies.

Carl Bake Rice Pudding

Ingredients:

1 Cup. water
1/2 Cup. Jasmine rice
2 Cups. Heavy cream or Light cream
½ Cup. Domino sugar if not sweet enough just add more sugar
½ Tsp. salt
¼ Tsp. McCormick Vanilla extract Cinnamon

1. Preheat oven to 325 degrees. Bring water to a boil in a small saucepan. Reduce heat to low. Add rice; simmer 5 minutes. Drain well.
2. Return rice to saucepan. Add milk, sugar and salt. Heat until just warm. Pour into 1 ½-quart baking dish.
3. Bake, 30 minutes, until thickened, 1 ¾-2 hours. Serve warm or chilled. Sprinkle with cinnamon before serving.

Three Flavor Pound Cake

3 Cups. Domino sugar
1 Cup. Land O lake butter
½ Cup. Crisco solid
5 Egg-lands eggs
3 Cup. Silk cake flour
1 Cup. Upstate farm whole milk
1 Tsp. McCormick Coconut extract, Butter extract, Vanilla extract
1 Tsp. Clabber Girl baking powder

Preheat oven to 350 degrees

Spray Bundt with Wilton baking spray or cake pan. Use an electric mixer. In a large bowl combine butter, shortening and sugar, Coconut extract, Butter extract, Vanilla extract and eggs 1 at a time. In medium bowl mix together, flour and baking powder. Gradually alternating flour and milk. Pour batter into ready Bundt pan bake at 350 degrees for 1- ½ hours. If done insert a wooden toothpick in the middle. Let cool on a wire rack.

Glaze for pound cake:

1 Cup. Domino sugar
½ Cup. Water
1 Tsp. Coconut extract, Butter extract, Vanilla extract.

Take a nonstick pot put sugar and water and coconut extract, butter extract, vanilla extract in the pot and bring to a boil. Pour ½ over Pound cake when remove from oven. Let cool on a wire rack pour the rest of the glaze on the pound cake.

Peanut Butter Sandwich Cookies

Ingredients:

1 Cup. Land O lake butter
1 Cup. Domino light brown sugar
1 Cup. Jif Peanut butter
3 Cups. Pillsbury flour or Gold Medal flour two of the best flour to use
2 Tsp. Baking soda
1 Cup. Domino sugar
2 Egg-land eggs
1 Tsp. McCormick Vanilla extract
¼ Tsp. Salt

Combine:

Cream butter, sugar, brown sugar, eggs, vanilla extract, peanut butter in a large bowl with an electric mixer until fluffy. In another bowl mix flour, salt, baking soda with a whist then put into creamed mixture.

Form mixture into 1-inch balls. Place 2 inches apart on parchment paper cookie sheet; press dough by making a crisscross pattern with a fork. Bake at 350 degrees for 10 minutes. Let cool on a wire rack until filling is made.

Filling:

½ Cup. Jif peanut butter
1 Tsp. McCormick vanilla extract
3 Cups. Domino confectioners' sugar
4 Tbsp. Upstate farm whole milk

Blend all ingredients together.

Key Lime Pie

The crust:

About 18 Vanilla Wafers
¼ Cup. Domino sugar
½ Tsp. ground cinnamon
5 Tbsp. Land O lake butter, melted

Filling:

4 extra-large egg yolks, lightly beaten egg-lands
1 can (14 oz. Carnation sweet condensed milk
1 ½ Tsp. grated lime zest
½ Cup. lime juice (from 3 or 4 lime
The Garnish with sweetened whipped cream

Preheat oven to 350 degrees

Use a food processor and process to crumbs. You should have 1 ¼ Cups. Mix the crumbs, sugar and cinnamon together in a bowl. Pour on the butter and mixture until the crumbs into are evenly moistened. Press the crumbs into the bottom and up the sides of an 8-inch spring form pan. Set aside.

Make the filling by whisking together the yolks, condensed milk, zest, and juice in a bowl. Pour the mixture into the crumb crust and bake for 20 to 25 minutes, or until the edges and the center are just set.

Pull the pie out of the oven and let cool to room temperature: Then chill it in the refrigerator. Slice into wedges and serve with cool whipped topping.

2 Layer pound cake

Ingredients:

3 sticks Land O lake butter unsalted
3 egg-Land eggs
2 Cups. Domino sugar
3 ½ Cup. Silk cake flour
2 Tsp. McCormick Vanilla extract
3 Tsp. Clabber Girl baking powder
1 ¼ Cup. Upstate farm whole milk

Prepare:

In a large bowl cream butter, sugar beat until fluffy. Add flavoring and eggs 1 at a time. Use an electric mixer on medium speed. Wet ingredients. For the dry ingredients. In a medium bowl combine cake flour, baking powder. With a whisk alternate flour mixture and milk. Bake at 325 degrees for 25-30 minutes put a wooden toothpick in the center of the cake if done let cake cool for 10 minutes.

Frosting:

2 Cups. Domino confectioners' sugar
1 stick Land O lake butter, softened
1 8oz. Philadelphia cream cheese
1 Tsp. McCormick Vanilla extract

Combine first 4 ingredients. Add remaining ingredients until frosting forms peaks.

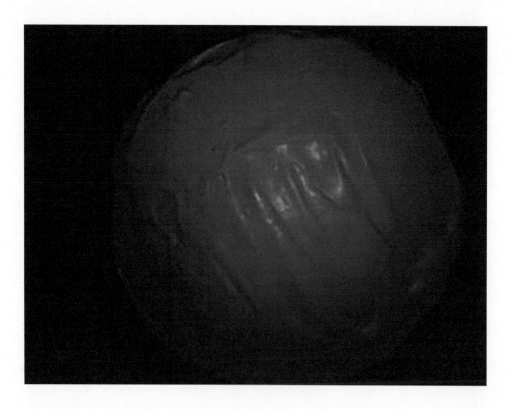

Printed in the United States
By Bookmasters